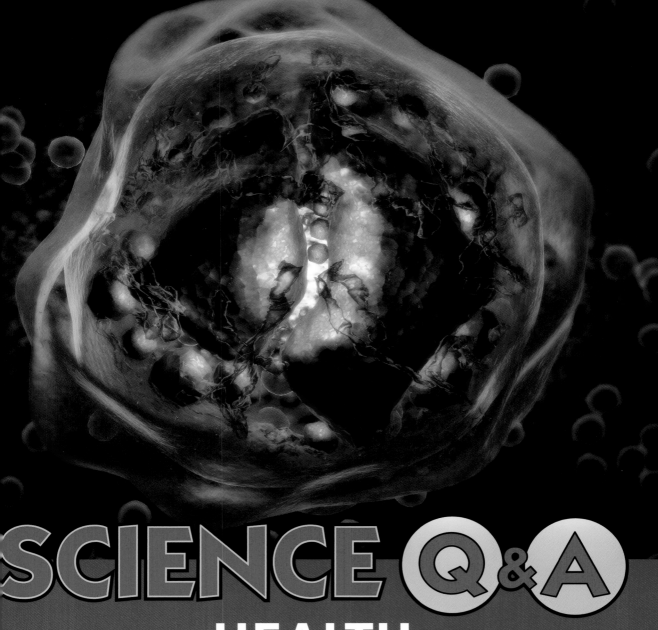

SCIENCE Q&A

HEALTH

— Celeste A. Peters —

Weigl Publishers Inc.

Published by Weigl Publishers Inc.
350 5th Avenue, Suite 3304, PMB 6G
New York, NY 10118-0069

Website: www.weigl.com

Library of Congress Cataloging-in-Publication Data

Peters, Celeste.
 Health : Science Q & A / Celeste Peters.
    p. cm.
 Includes index.
 ISBN 978-1-59036-948-7 (hard cover : alk. paper) -- ISBN 978-1-59036-949-4 (soft cover : alk. paper)
 1. Health--Juvenile literature. I. Title.
 RA777.P48 2009
 613--dc22
                              2008003821

Printed in China
1 2 3 4 5 6 7 8 9 0 12 11 10 09 08

Project Coordinator
Heather Hudak

Design
Terry Paulhus

Photo credits

All images supplied by Getty Images.

CONTENTS

What is good health?

Have you ever wondered what it means to be healthy, why you sometimes get sick, or how doctors can treat certain ailments?

How you feel has a big impact on your life. It is easy to run laps around the schoolyard when you are feeling well. If you try doing the same thing when you have an upset stomach, you may not make it very far. You need to be alert and healthy to do your best.

The human body has amazing ways to fight off disease and remain in top shape, but you must take care of it. The ancient Greeks believed that good health means having both a fit body and a fit mind. Your brain works better if your body is in good shape. Your body suffers fewer aches and pains if your mind is free of **stress**. Personal cleanliness, regular exercise, and nutritious food are keys to good health. They help your body maintain something called **homeostasis**.

Why is it important to have a healthy diet?

Everyone knows that people starve to death if they do not eat. Did you know that you can eat plenty and still have poor health?

find it quick

Learn more about vitamins, minerals, and healthy eating by visiting **http://www.nutritionexplorations. org/kids/nutrition-main.asp**.

What you eat is just as important as how much you eat. The key to a healthy diet is eating a variety of foods. Food contains **nutrients** like vitamins and minerals. Vitamins and minerals do not supply any energy in food, but they are needed for the body to work properly.

Variety in the diet is important because not all foods contain the same nutrients. Imagine you only ate oranges all day. You would get plenty of vitamin C but none of the mineral calcium. If you ate only fish, you would have a great deal of vitamin A but no vitamin C.

Certain vitamins and minerals are so important that a person can become very sick if he or she does not eat enough of them. Before this was known, sailors at sea went for long periods without eating fresh fruits and vegetables. As a result, they often became sick and died from a disease called scurvy. Scurvy is caused by a lack of vitamin C.

■ Canned Atlantic sardines are a rich source of calcium. They have soft bones that can be eaten, unlike fish with solid bones.

What healthy bones you have

The body needs calcium to grow and maintain strong bones. The best sources of calcium are milk, cheese, yogurt, canned fish with bones, and dark green vegetables. So, eat your spinach.

Science Q&A | Q | Health

What can exercise do for you?

Are you a couch potato? If not, exercise probably helps keep you healthy.

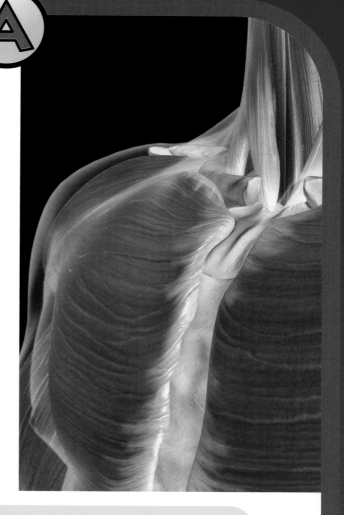

Regular exercise improves a person's posture, works off mental stress, and helps a person sleep well at night. Best of all, regular exercise helps keep people fit. This is important because a fit body works best.

Several changes take place in the body when a person exercises regularly. Muscles and bones grow stronger. The heart becomes a better pump. The lungs work more efficiently, which means that they can deliver more oxygen to the body. The body relies on oxygen to turn the food a person eats into the energy muscles need to function.

■ Muscles are made of tiny fibers. Each muscle fiber is thinner than a hair.

Here is your challenge!

Your muscles need more energy when you exercise. They need extra oxygen to make energy. How do your muscles get more oxygen?

1. Take your pulse. Record how many times your heart beats in one minute. Write down how many times you inhale in one minute.
2. Run in place or do some other fast exercise for two minutes.
3. Repeat step 1.

How did your body transport more oxygen to its muscles? (Hint: Blood picks up oxygen from the air as it passes through your lungs.)

How does hygiene affect your health?

Hygiene means staying healthy by being clean. Germs stay away from well-scrubbed, clean bodies. You can can keep germs away by washing regularly, especially after you sweat.

find it quick

To learn more about how to keep clean, visit **www.cyh.com**. Click on "Kids' Health," and search "hygiene."

■ Bathing everyday helps control acne, body odor, and other hygiene issues caused by germs.

Even though germs are unable to get through the skin, they can cause sore, red pimples on a person's face, neck, or back. This is called acne. Acne is caused by a natural oil produced by the skin. This oil mixes with sweat and dead skin to form an oily layer on the skin. Germs invade this layer and cause acne to flare up. Washing with soap and warm water a few times each day helps to keep the oily layer from building up.

Germs and a type of **bacteria** called plaque are to blame for cavities and bad breath. Plaque lives on teeth and eats the sugars left behind after a person eats. Plaque makes acid that eats right through tooth enamel, the hard substance that covers teeth. This acid causes cavities and bad breath. Brushing and flossing help to keep plaque under control.

Making a stink

Strenuous exercise causes people to sweat. Body odor is easy to control with soap and a shower or bath.

What happens to your body when you sleep?

When you do not get enough sleep for several nights in a row, do you sometimes become sick? There is a good reason why this happens.

The **immune system** becomes more active while a person sleeps. It goes into high gear, fighting off germs that have invaded the body. If a person does not sleep long enough, the immune system does not have a chance to do its job. The germs may win the battle.

Sleep gives the body and mind a chance to rest. Well-rested muscles recover more quickly from exercise and grow stronger. Not getting enough sleep can cause the brain to work slowly. This will affect learning and behavior.

About 8 to 12 hours of sleep per night is best for children. Adults need seven to eight hours of sleep. Newborn babies sleep an average of 16 to 18 hours per day. Teenagers need about nine hours of sleep every night. Older adults need as much sleep as younger adults, but they tend to sleep less at night. Elderly people are more likely to suffer from sleep disorders, such as insomnia. People with insomnia have trouble falling asleep or staying asleep.

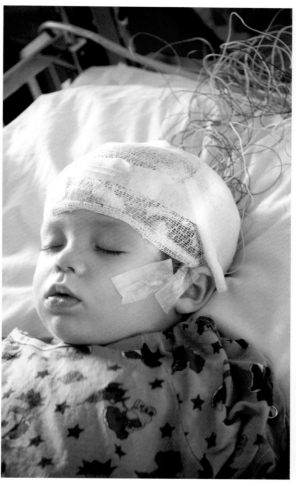

■ An electroencephalogram (EEG) is a test that measures brain activity. It can be used to treat sleep disorders.

Dream on

People dream every night. On average, a person has 1,825 dreams per year. That adds up to 136,875 dreams by the time a person is 75 years old.

What is pain?

Nobody likes to be in pain. People try to avoid being in pain by staying healthy and safe, but sometimes, it cannot be avoided.

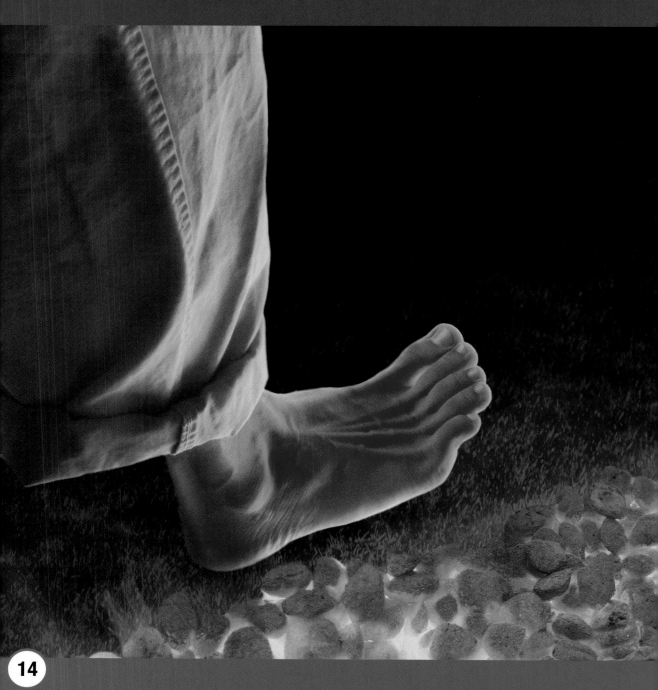

Believe it or not, you need pain. It can save your life. Pain is the body's warning system. It sends a message loud and clear when something is wrong. Imagine what it would be like if people could not sense pain. If they cut themselves, they could bleed to death without realizing they were hurt. If their clothes caught on fire, they might not know before they were seriously burned.

When something damages the body, the **cells** in the injured area send out chemicals. These chemicals activate nearby nerves, the fibers that send messages between the brain and the rest of the body. These nerves send an urgent message to the brain. Almost instantly, the person feels pain in the injured area. At the same time, the brain sends a return message to the affected area that says, "Get out of there."

If the pain is caused by an outside force, such as heat from the burner on a stove, the person will immediately pull away from whatever is hurting them.

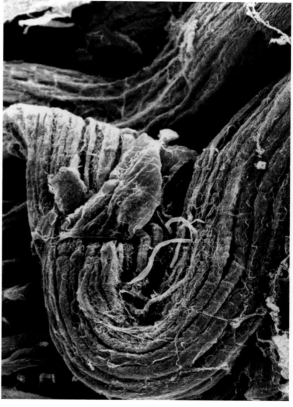

■ Nerves are made up of fibers, like tiny ropes. These ropes communicate with the brain, allowing people to feel.

Pain from inside the body, such as a stomach ache or a headache, can be a signal from the body that something is wrong.

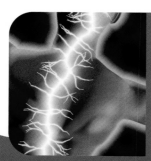

Ouch! That's fast!

The messages that go back and forth between an injured body part and the brain travel at up to 330 feet (100 meters) per second.

How does the body defend against germs?

Millions of germs try to invade your body every day. Germs are tiny organisms that cause disease. You cannot see germs, but they are in the air you breathe and on the food you eat.

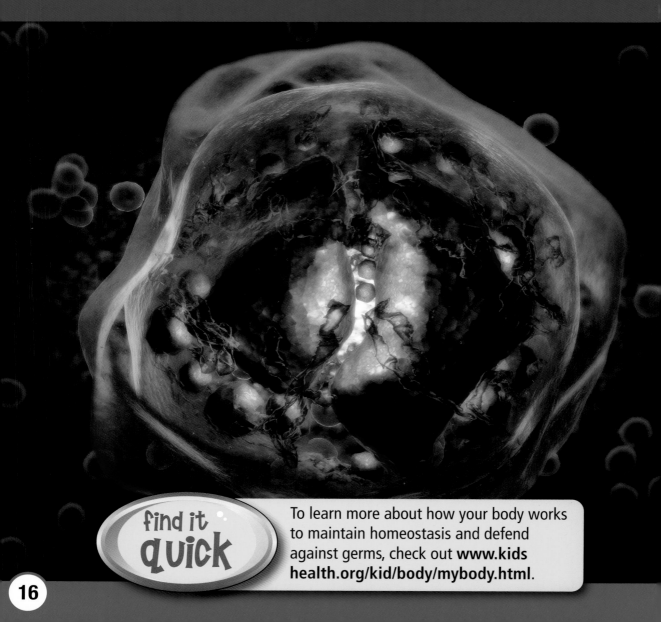

find it quick

To learn more about how your body works to maintain homeostasis and defend against germs, check out **www.kids health.org/kid/body/mybody.html**.

The body's biggest defense against germs is skin. The only way germs can get past skin is through cuts, scratches, and openings, including the nose, mouth, eyes, and ears.

The body has other defenses to stop germs that get through the skin. The nose and mouth trap germs with a sticky substance called mucus. Ears have wax in them to trap germs. Tears in the eyes wash germs out and contain a chemical that kills bacteria.

If germs get past all these defenses, they face the immune system. White blood cells called phagocytes and lymphocytes are the immune system's most powerful weapons. Phagocytes flow through the blood and eat germs. Lymphocytes launch an army of antibodies. Each antibody kills a different type of germ. It covers the germ in a substance that attracts phagocytes. The body remembers how to make the antibody for each type of germ. If the same type of germ comes back, the

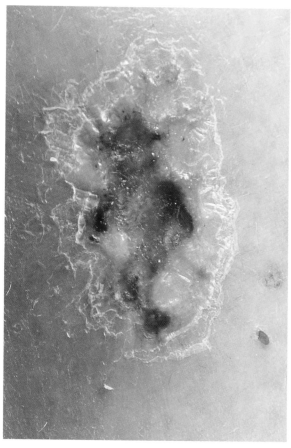

■ Scabs keep germs from getting through cuts in the skin. Special blood cells, called platelets, stick together to form a scab over the cut.

body can fight it off easily. This protection from disease is called immunity.

Super sneeze

Sneezing removes things that tickle the inside of your nose. Germs tickle by making the lining of your nose swell. A sneeze sends the invaders flying out of your nose at up to 100 miles (160 kilometers) per hour.

How does homeostasis protect your body?

In order for a person to stay healthy, the environment in his or her body should always remain the same. The body's temperature must stay close to 98.6° Fahrenheit (37° Celsius). The amount of blood and other fluids must not suddenly increase or decrease too much.

Homeostasis is the process that keeps the environment inside your body the same when possible.

Imagine it is a freezing-cold day. You have been outside building a snowman for an hour. Your hands, feet, and face are cold. Why? Homeostasis is at work protecting you. All your warm blood is flowing around important organs such as your heart and lungs. In addition, homeostasis might make your muscles twitch or shiver. This creates heat, so your body can stay at the right temperature.

Homeostasis protects you if you go outside on a very hot day. It cools you down by activating **glands**. This makes you sweat. Sometimes, homeostasis makes your temperature rise. When you have a fever, the heat helps your body destroy the germs that are making you ill.

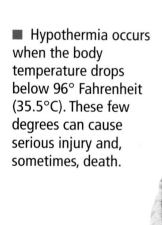

■ Hypothermia occurs when the body temperature drops below 96° Fahrenheit (35.5°C). These few degrees can cause serious injury and, sometimes, death.

Don't sweat it

Women actually have more sweat glands than men. However, men sweat more because their glands are more active than women's.

How does disease spread?

Diseases are caused by germs. When germs get past all of a person's defenses, they make that person sick. Many diseases can be passed between people. These diseases are contagious.

find it quick

For information about germs and disease, check out **www.amnh.org/ nationalcenter/infection**.

Many objects have germs on them. People should wash their hands frequently to avoid getting sick.

Imagine you are in an elevator. Someone sneezes without covering his or her mouth. Millions of germs fly out into the air—the very air you are breathing. Some people in Asia wear masks when they are ill. This keeps germs from spreading. Surgeons wear a mask in the operating room so that germs in their breath will not infect their patients.

Germs can get into food and water. This gives them a free ride into the stomach. There are several ways a person can protect against these germs. Wash raw fruits and vegetables thoroughly before eating them. Eat only well-cooked meat. Boil untreated water before using it.

■ People cover their mouth when they sneeze or cough. This leaves their hand covered in germs. The germs are left on anything the person touches.

Most water in the United States and Canada is treated, which means that harmful bacteria, dirt, and unpleasant tastes and smells have been removed.

Buzz off

Insects are known to spread some of the world's deadliest diseases. Millions of people die every year from malaria, a disease spread by mosquitoes. In the 1300s, the bubonic plague spread to humans through fleas and killed 25 million people in Europe. That was one third of the continent's population.

What are common childhood diseases?

There are several diseases that children are especially vulnerable to. These diseases include chicken pox, mumps, and measles.

Chicken pox is a virus that begins as a rash. The rash turns into clear, fluid-filled bumps. The bumps itch and form scabs. It is not good to scratch the bumps. Germs from the fingers can infect the bumps and leave scars. Chicken pox can give people a mild fever, make them feel tired, or cause them to lose their appetite. In rare cases, it can even be fatal.

Mumps can begin with an earache, fever, fatigue, and loss of appetite. Soon, the fever goes up, and the glands just below the ears swell. The swelling makes it painful to chew or swallow.

Sometimes mumps lead to life-threatening diseases and can prevent men from fathering babies.

Small blue dots with red rings around them inside the mouth are a sure sign of rubeola, the severe form of measles. When the dots go away, the person's temperature rises, and a red rash covers the body. Rubeola can cause pneumonia, deafness, or brain damage. It is much worse than rubella, the mild form of measles.

■ When a cell is affected by measles, blood cells surround it and destroy the virus.

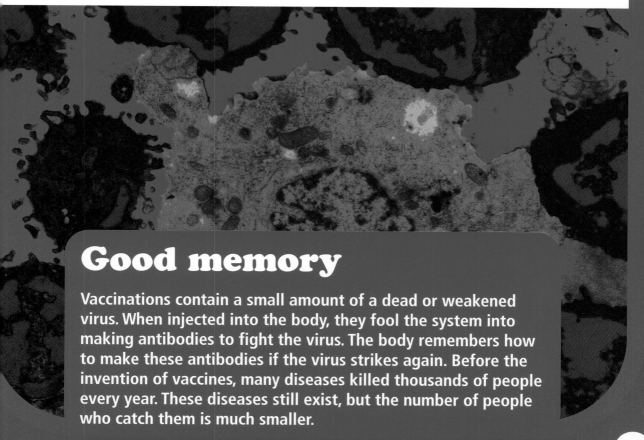

Good memory

Vaccinations contain a small amount of a dead or weakened virus. When injected into the body, they fool the system into making antibodies to fight the virus. The body remembers how to make these antibodies if the virus strikes again. Before the invention of vaccines, many diseases killed thousands of people every year. These diseases still exist, but the number of people who catch them is much smaller.

What causes allergies and asthma?

Millions of people in North America have allergies. This means their immune system overreacts to substances that are usually harmless, such as dust or certain foods. These substances are called allergens.

find it quick

To learn more about asthma and lung health, surf to **www.lung.ca/children/index_kids.html**.

When the immune system mistakes something, such as a peanut, for an invader, it tries to destroy it by creating chemicals that signal a battle is about to begin. As a side effect, the chemicals trigger symptoms, or signs, of an allergy.

The allergy symptoms a person experiences depend on where the chemicals are released in the body. When the chemicals are released in the eyes and nose, they cause sneezing, runny nose, and itchy eyes. When they are released in the stomach, they cause diarrhea and vomiting. When they are released in the skin, they cause swelling, redness, and hives. If the chemicals are released in the lungs, they cause swelling inside the breathing tubes. The chemicals can create a great deal of mucus. This can trigger an asthma attack.

People with asthma are often allergic to pollen, animal **dander**, dust mites, molds, or certain foods. Allergens are not the only triggers. Exercise, smoke, cold air, perfume, aspirin, and **food additives** can cause an asthma attack.

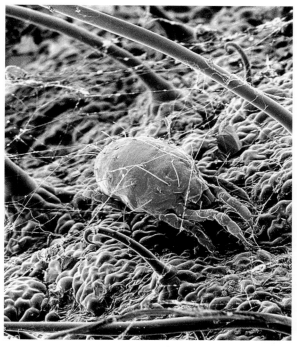

■ Dust mites are a common allergen. They are so small that they can only be seen with a microscope. Dust mites are found in mattresses, clothing, sofas, and other soft, warm areas around the home.

During an asthma attack, the breathing tubes leading to the lungs 'twitch' and narrow. This makes it very difficult to breathe.

Take a breather

More than half of the people who have asthma are between the ages of 2 and 17.

What are some different types of medicines?

Your immune system is very good at fighting off germs. Sometimes, it cannot do the job on its own. When you get sick, your immune system needs help.

Antibiotics are medicines that weaken and kill bacteria. Bacteria cause infections, such as earaches and strep throat, among other things. It is important to finish all the antibiotics the doctor prescribes, even if you begin to feel better. If a person stops taking it too soon, some bacteria will remain in the body. These will multiply and make the person sick again.

When a person has an allergic reaction, a chemical called histamine is loose in the body. It is triggering the nose to run and the eyes to water. An antihistamine is a medicine that prevents the histamine from acting.

Analgesics are a type of painkiller. There are two types of analgesics. An anti-inflammatory analgesic, such as aspirin, dissolves in the stomach and enters the bloodstream. The bloodstream carries it to the place that hurts. Once there, the analgesic stops production of the chemical that signals the brain to sense pain. An opioid analgesic, such as morphine, is much stronger. It goes straight to the **spinal cord** and brain to block pain messages. Stronger yet is the anesthetic used during surgery. It makes it very difficult for one nerve cell to send messages to the next, so pain signals never reach the brain, and the person blacks out.

The stomach uses acid to break down food and kill germs, but too much acid in the stomach is bad. It can contribute to the pain of heartburn and make **ulcers** worse. Antacids are chemicals that combine with acids and take away their power to do harm.

■ Some antibiotics, such as penicillin, are made from substances in molds that protect the mold from bacteria.

Pepper patch

Peppers and other spicy foods cause heartburn in some people. However, creams made from some types of peppers are thought to help ease pain from arthritis.

Why do diabetics need insulin?

Some people with diabetes face the challenge of giving themselves an injection of medicine every day to stay healthy. They must have daily shots of insulin.

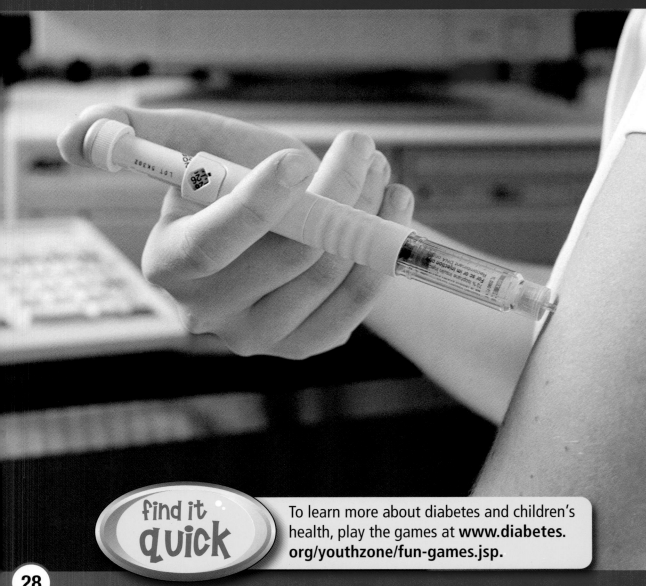

find it quick

To learn more about diabetes and children's health, play the games at **www.diabetes.org/youthzone/fun-games.jsp.**

Insulin is a chemical that helps sugar enter the cells of the body. Cells need sugar because it provides the energy that they need to work. Without insulin to help process sugar, cells starve, and sugar builds up in the blood.

Insulin is produced by an organ called the pancreas. Some people have a pancreas that cannot make enough insulin. They have a disease called Type I diabetes. They must take daily insulin shots and follow a special diet.

Not all diabetics take injections of insulin. Most diabetics have Type II diabetes, and their pancreas creates enough insulin. However, their body is unable to make the insulin work as it should. These people can usually treat diabetes with exercise and a special diet. A few must take insulin injections.

Untreated diabetes can cause heart disease, stroke, kidney disease, blindness, nerve damage, and difficulty fighting off infections. It is the sixth-leading cause of death in the United States.

■ People with diabetes can test their blood-sugar level with a small monitor. The monitor measures the amount of sugar in a drop of blood from the fingertip.

Science Q&A   **Q**   Health

What are autoimmune diseases?

The human body is like a very complex computer. It is made up of many parts that perform different functions to keep us healthy. Certain parts can malfunction, which can cause serious problems for the body.

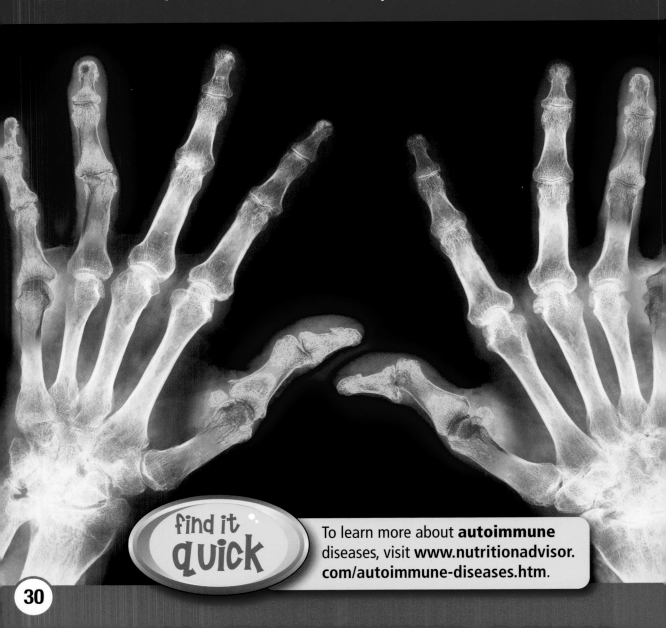

find it quick

To learn more about **autoimmune** diseases, visit **www.nutritionadvisor. com/autoimmune-diseases.htm**.

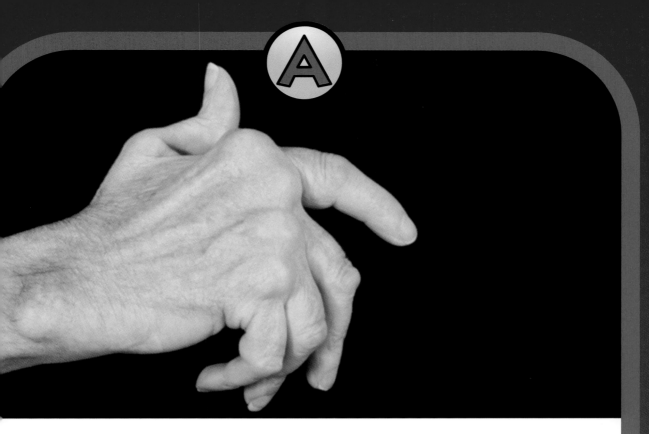

Sometimes, the body's immune system makes a huge mistake. It begins attacking perfectly good body tissue. No one knows why it does this. The immune system simply considers this tissue an invader. This results in autoimmune diseases.

Rheumatoid arthritis is the most common autoimmune disease. It begins some time between childhood and middle age. The immune system suddenly begins attacking body tissue in joints. It sends out large numbers of white blood cells to do battle in fingers, toes, knees,

■ Rheumatoid arthritis can cause joints, including knuckles, to become deformed.

shoulders, elbows, the spine, and other joints. This causes swelling and pain, and it slowly destroys the joints.

There are several other autoimmune diseases. Lupus attacks tissues in the skin, blood vessels, heart, and kidneys. Multiple sclerosis attacks the nerves. Some scientists now believe that Type I diabetes is caused by an autoimmune disease that attacks insulin-making cells in the pancreas.

Aches and rain

Some people with arthritis can tell when wet weather is on the way. Their joints ache more.

How does heart disease develop?

Do you eat potato chips, hamburgers, deep-fried chicken, pizza, or ice cream regularly? These foods might appeal to your taste buds, but they could be harming your heart. Heart disease is a condition that prevents the heart from working properly.

find it quick

To learn how you can keep your heart healthy, check out **www.healthyfridge. org/justforkids.html**.

Your heart is a special type of muscle. It pumps blood to muscles and organs throughout your body. The blood leaves the heart through tubes called arteries. Coronary arteries bring blood to the heart muscle itself. If something blocks a coronary artery, the heart does not receive the oxygen-rich blood it needs to work. The result is a heart attack. If something blocks an artery leading to the brain, the result is a stroke.

Plaque is the main cause of blocked arteries. This is not the same plaque that builds up on your teeth. This plaque is quite different. It is a fatty substance that builds up on the inside of arteries. As it builds up, it leaves less and less room for blood to flow through.

There are two things a person can do to help prevent the buildup of plaque—exercise and limit the amount of saturated fats eaten.

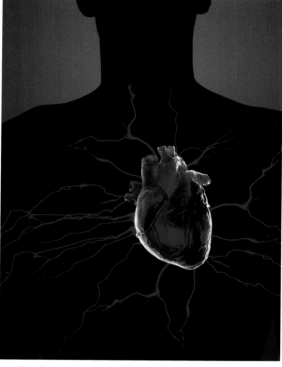

■ The heart pumps about 1.32 gallons (5 liters) of blood every minute.

Saturated fats are found in foods such as red meat, poultry, dairy products, deep-fried foods, coconut oil, and palm oil.

Here is your challenge!

Can you guess how many times your heart will beat during your lifetime? The heart beats about 70 times each minute. This means that it beats 4,200 times per hour, 100,800 times per day, and 36,792,000 times per year. How many times will it beat if you live to be the following ages?

    a) 70 years old
    b) 80 years old
    c) 100 years old

Answers: a) 2.5 billion, b) 2.9 billion, c) nearly 3.7 billion

What is cancer?

More than one million people in the United States are diagnosed with cancer each year. More than 500,000 people in the United States die from cancer every year. It is the second-leading cause of death in the United States.

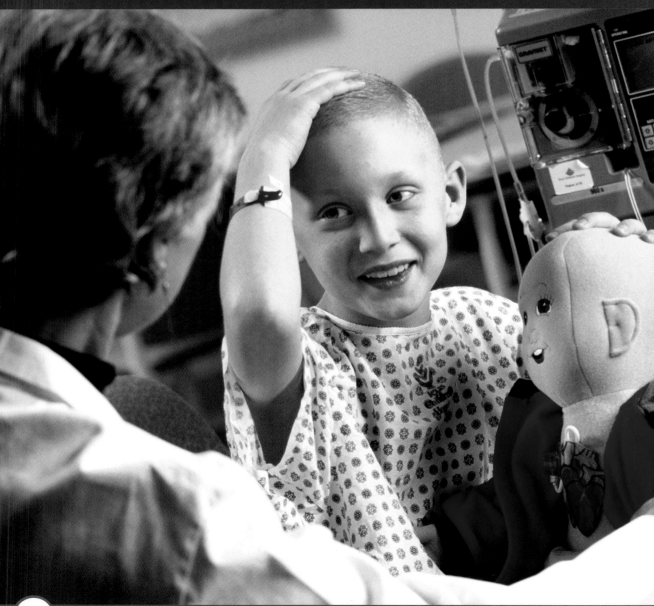

Cancer is a disease that affects the cells of the body. A human begins as a single cell, the basic building block of most living material. This cell grows and splits into two separate cells. These cells divide and become four cells, then eight cells, then sixteen, and so on. This rapid multiplication continues until there are the trillions of cells that make up an adult body. Then, the process slows down. The cells of an adult normally divide only when new cells are needed to replace old ones.

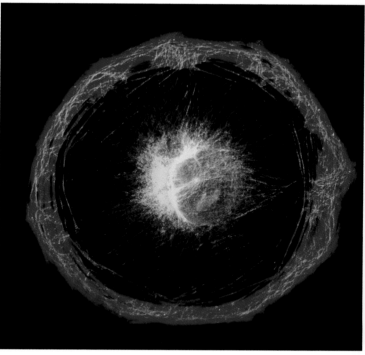

■ Cancer cells spread to other parts of the body because they do not stick together like normal cells.

Sometimes, a cell grows and multiplies out of control. All of the extra cells it creates clump together in a lump called a tumor. If cells break away from the tumor, they can spread to other places in the body and start more tumors. When this happens, a person is said to have cancer. Unless the spread of tumors is stopped, these lumps begin to interfere with the proper working of other tissue and organs in the body.

One form of cancer, called leukemia, does not usually form tumors. These cancer cells involve blood and blood-forming organs in the body, such as **bone marrow**. The cells move through tissue in the body and can group together.

Tumor rumor

Malignant tumors cause cancer. Tumors that do not spread to other parts of the body are called benign tumors. These are rarely life-threatening.

How do cigarettes and alcohol harm your body?

You may know people who smoke or drink alcohol. Although you cannot see the effects inside your body, these things are very bad for your health.

Cigarette smoke contains 4,000 chemicals. Two hundred of these are known poisons. They can cause a variety of health problems, including bad breath, loss of smell and taste, and stained teeth and fingers. Cigarettes are known to cause many deadly health conditions, such as emphysema, high blood pressure, stroke, heart disease, and cancer. Smoking causes about 440,000 deaths in the United States every year.

Once a person begins smoking, it is very hard to stop. Cigarettes can become an addiction. This means the body starts to depend on them. One out of every three young people who experiment with smoking is addicted by the age of 20.

Alcohol goes straight from the stomach into the bloodstream. Blood carries it to other parts of the body. When alcohol reaches the brain, it can affect how a person thinks and acts.

The liver is the organ that rids the body of alcohol. Alcohol abuse can cause damage to the liver, heart, and nervous system, as well as loss of memory, low vitamin levels, and changes in behavior.

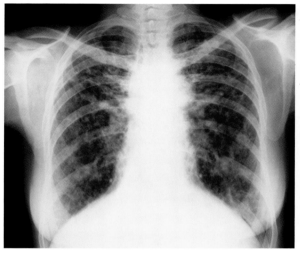

■ Healthy lungs are clean and can breathe easily.

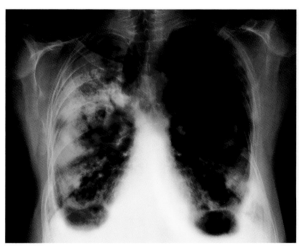

■ Smoking damages the lungs by filling them with chemicals, including tar. These chemicals stay in the lungs even after the smoke is exhaled.

Put this in your pipe

Smoking kills more people each year than murder, fire, suicide, alcohol abuse, drug abuse, car crashes, and AIDS combined.

Why is too much sunshine dangerous to your health?

Most people enjoy spending time outside on sunny days. Beaches are often crowded in the summer with people trying to get a suntan. The Sun creates energy for almost all life on Earth, but it can do great harm to people.

find it quick

To learn more about sun safety, check out **http://nsc.org/library/facts/agrisun.htm.**

Sunshine contains ultraviolet (UV) rays. People cannot see these rays, but they can do great harm to the body by causing sunburns. They are especially dangerous if a person spends a great deal of time outside without UV protection.

Every time a person gets a sunburn, it damages the skin. Sunburn can cause wrinkles at an early age. It can also cause skin cancer. More than 500,000 people in the United States develop skin cancer every year.

It is important to protect yourself from the Sun's harmful rays. Wear clothing that covers as much skin as possible. Sunscreen is a chemical that prevents UV rays from reaching the skin. Cover exposed skin with sunscreen that has an SPF (Sun protection factor) of at least 30.

Exposure to UV rays over many years can cloud the lenses in the eyes and make it difficult to see. These clouds are called cataracts. Sometimes, a great deal of UV rays enter the eyes in a short period of time. This can cause temporary blindness.

Here is your challenge!

Most skin damage from the Sun occurs before a person reaches 18 years of age. This type of damage can lead to skin cancer, the most common form of cancer in the United States. However, skin cancer can be treated. If you know what to look for, you can stop skin cancer. Each year, have a doctor check your skin for any sign of cancer. Between visits, check your body for unusual spots each month. The following outlines how to do this.

1. Use a mirror to check your face, neck, and shoulders.
2. To check your head, use a hairdryer to blow hair away from the scalp. This will allow you to see better.
3. Check your hands, feet, and nails. Be sure to look between your fingers and toes.
4. Stand in front of a mirror to look for spots on the front of your body.
5. Angle a second mirror so that you can see the back of your body.

If you notice any unusual spots, visit your doctor for advice. For more information about skin cancer, visit ww.skincancer.org.

How do thoughts and feelings affect your health?

Have you ever worried about something so much that it made you sick to your stomach? When you do not feel well, do you watch television or read a book to take your mind off what ails you?

find it quick

For information about how to cope with different emotions, visit **www.kidshealth. org/kid/feeling/index.html**.

The mind and body are connected. This is particularly obvious when people are under a great deal of mental stress. Mental stress is the tense feeling you get when you take a test or perform in front of an audience. It feels like you have butterflies in your stomach. Mental stress can do many things to the body. It can make muscles twitch and the heart beat faster. Sometimes, mental stress can be a good thing, but too much mental stress over long periods of time can cause heart attacks, **depression**, and stomach ulcers.

On the other hand, positive thoughts and feelings can have a good effect on health. Happy people may be healthier and live longer than unhappy people. Love and friendship can be important. People who are surrounded by good friends, a loving family, and pets may be healthier than lonely people.

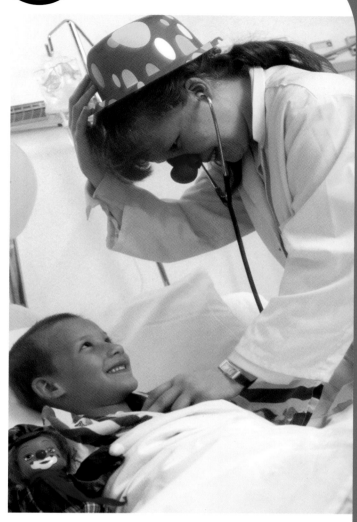

■ People who are happy in life are healthier. Members of the International Center for Humor and Health visit hospitals to make patients laugh and recover faster.

Don't worry, be happy

Stress is caused by the way a person reacts to a situation. If a person reacts negatively, stress builds up. Positive reactions ease stress. So, look on the bright side.

What are eating disorders?

Did you know that you can diet yourself to death? People with eating disorders, or severe disturbances in their eating habits, sometimes do.

find it quick

For more information about learning disorders, visit **http://pbskids.org/ itsmylife/body/eatingdisorders**.

Most people with eating disorders are female. No matter how thin they are, they want to be thinner. People with the eating disorder anorexia nervosa actually fear being fat. They eat very little, and they exercise a great deal to work off the food they eat. People with the eating disorder bulimia nervosa do not starve themselves. Instead, they eat huge amounts, and then they make themselves vomit to get rid of the food they have eaten.

This over-dieting does several things to the body. It makes nails, hair, and bones brittle. It stops **menstruation** and can lead to depression, worrying, and substance abuse. Most importantly, it damages vital organs, such as the heart, kidneys, and brain.

People cannot catch an eating disorder, but they may inherit one. Eating disorders seem to run in families. A person may also develop an eating disorder if they place too much importance on their looks.

■ Models, ballerinas, and gymnasts may be at increased risk of developing eating disorders. They often feel they must be thin to be successful.

Eat up

Anorexia nervosa can start as early as age seven. Most people who develop this eating disorder do so between ages 11 and 14.

Health Careers

Family Doctor

A family doctor is the first health care professional most people see when they have a medical problem. The doctor must talk to and examine the patient, looking for clues to what is wrong. Once the problem is identified, the doctor suggests the right treatment for the patient to get well.

Family doctors treat patients of all ages. Doctors go to medical school and train in clinics and hospitals. They gain experience treating many different ailments.

Physical Therapist

Physical therapists help people recover from an injury, illness, or disability. They create training programs for people who have trouble moving and functioning properly. Massage and developing exercise programs are some of the ways that physical therapists help people improve their health.

To become a physiotherapist, a person must first complete a science degree from a university. Then, the person can begin training in an office, or continue his or her education to specialize in a certain area, such as sports injuries, head and spinal cord injuries, and working with children.

To learn more about health careers, visit **http://bhpr.hrsa. gov/kidscareers/about.htm**.

Young scientists at work
Test Your Knowledge

You can probably answer the questions using only the book, your own experiences, and your common sense.

Fact:
Your heart is made of a type of muscle that can work for longer periods of time that the other muscles in your body.

Test:
You will need a watch or clock with a second hand to do this experiment. Make a tight fist with your hand, then relax your hand. Repeat this tightening and relaxing movement 70 times per minute. This is how many times your heart beats every minute.

Predict:
What will happen to the muscles in your hand after a while? Your heart does not become tired the way your hand does because it is made of a different type of muscle.

Fact:
Your body has many built-in defenses against germs.

Test:
Which of the following are defenses against germs?

bad breath	smelly feet
earwax	tears
stomach acid	sweat
a sneeze	antibodies

Answers:
Earwax, stomach acid, a sneeze, tears, and antibodies are defenses against germs. Bad breath, smelly feet, and sweat are not.

Take a health survey

Answer the questions about smoking, then check out
www.tobaccofreekids.org/research/ to learn more.

1. Are you a smoker, or have you ever tried smoking a cigarette?

2. Have most people your age tried cigarettes?

3. Will it be okay to smoke cigarettes when you are in high school?

4. Is there a relationship between teenage smoking, drinking, and drug abuse?

5. Do most adults smoke cigarettes?

STATISTICS: Everyday, about 4,000 children in the United States try their first cigarette. About 1,000 of these kids become addicted, daily smokers. Nicotine is a very addictive drug. A person can become addicted in only a few days after trying their first cigarette.

According to a study by the University of Michigan, 8.7 percent of eighth graders and 14.5 percent of tenth graders are smokers. About 21.6 percent of students are smokers by the time they leave high school. About thirty percent of youth smokers will die early from smoking related causes.

The U.S. Department of Health and Human Services says that teens between 12 and 17 years of age who smoke are 11 percent more likely to use illegal drugs and 16 percent more likely to drink heavily than those who do not smoke.

About 20 percent of adults, or about 45 million people, in the United States smoke.

Fast Facts

Babies have about 300 bones. Adults have only 206. As a person grows, some of the bones join together.

In healthy adults, three billion cells die every minute. However, living cells divide and replace most of the dead ones.

Water alone cannot wash away oily dirt on the skin. Water and oil are made of tiny bits called molecules that do not stick to one another. Soap molecules stick to both water and oil molecules. Soap makes a connection between the two and washes them away.

One of every three people sneezes at the sight of bright light. This trait is inherited from a parent.

The smallest living thing is a virus. More than 25 million viruses can fit on the head of a pin.

On average, women live longer than men.

Few people survive if their body temperature rises above 109° Fahrenheit (43°C). The highest body temperature on record is 115° Fahrenheit (46°C).

Today, many people take aspirin to relieve pain. Early American Indians chewed the bark of the willow tree. It contains the same chemical used to make aspirin.

There are five feelings that can prevent you from thinking clearly—hate, anger, hurt, fear, and romantic love.

Heart disease is the leading cause of death in North America.

Glossary

autoimmune: having immunity to tissue in one's own body

bacteria: one-celled organisms

bone marrow: tissue inside bones that forms into blood cells

cells: the basic building blocks of all living material

dander: scales from skin, hair, or feathers

depression: a medical condition that causes a person to feel sad

food additives: substances added to food, such as artificial color or flavor

glands: organs that produce and release substances needed by the body

homeostasis: the process that keeps the environment inside your body the same when possible

immune system: the network of cells and tissue that protects the body from harmful organisms

menstruation: monthly flow of blood from the lining of the uterus

nutrients: substances that help build tissue and give energy to the body

spinal cord: the large bundle of nerves inside the spine

stress: mental or emotional pressure

ulcers: sore spots that are accompanied by a loss of tissue

Index